FRIENDSHIP

PORTRAITS IN GOD'S FAMILY ALBUM

11 Studies for Individuals or Groups

STEVE & DEE BRESTIN

Harold Shaw Publishers • Wheaton, Illinois

ISBN 978-0-877-88287-9

Cover photo © 1994 by Luci Shaw

146502721

CONTENTS

INTRODUCTION

"Perfume and incense bring joy to the heart,
and the pleasantness of one's friend springs
from his earnest counsel." (Proverbs 27:9)

What strength, hope, and joy a close friendship can add to life! Yet rarely do men and women study the friendships of Scripture. Perhaps because of the great need for strengthening Christian marriages, believers have studied that relationship to the exclusion of others. Yet throughout the ages, God has used friends mightily to make an enormous difference in the lives of others. Therefore it seems prudent to study the male and female models God has provided, in his family album, of the kind of friends he calls us to be.

As you study, you will see a pattern—a repetition of the Christlike characteristics of commitment, unfailing kindness, and vulnerability. Solomon tells us that friends like this are very rare; yet, for those who are willing to mature in Christ, it is possible to emulate the examples God has provided. Whether you are a beginning or an advanced Bible student, make a commitment now to work hard and seriously. Help each other to maintain a high standard of study and obedience.

May the Lord help you to meet his standard for friendship.

Steve & Dee Brestin

HOW TO USE THIS STUDYGUIDE

Fisherman studyguides are based on the inductive approach to Bible study. Inductive study is discovery study; we discover what the Bible says as we ask questions about its content and search for answers. This is quite different from the process in which a teacher *tells* a group *about* the Bible and what it means and what to do about it. In inductive study God speaks directly to each of us through his Word.

A group functions best when a leader keeps the discussion on target, but this leader is neither the teacher nor the "answer person." A leader's responsibility is to *ask*—not *tell*. The answers come from the text itself as group members examine, discuss, and think together about the passage.

There are four kinds of questions in each study. The first is an *approach question*. Used before the Bible passage is read, this question breaks the ice and helps you focus on the topic of the Bible study. It begins to reveal where thoughts and feelings need to be transformed by Scripture.

Some of the earlier questions in each study are *observation questions* designed to help you find out basic facts—who, what, where, when, and how.

When you know what the Bible says you need to ask, *What does it mean?* These *interpretation questions* help you to discover the writer's basic message.

Application questions ask, *What does it mean to me?* They challenge you to live out the Scripture's life-transforming message.

Fisherman studyguides provide spaces between questions for jotting down responses and related questions you would like to raise in the group. Each group member should have a copy of the studyguide and may take a turn in leading the group.

For consistency, Fisherman guides are written from the *New International Version.* But a group should feel free to use the NIV or any other accurate, modern translation of the Bible such as the *New Living Translation,* the *New Revised Standard Version,* the *New Jerusalem Bible,* or the *Good News Bible.* (Other paraphrases of the Bible may be referred to when additional help is needed.) Bible commentaries should not be brought to a Bible study because they tend to dampen discussion and keep people from thinking for themselves.

SUGGESTIONS FOR GROUP LEADERS

1. Read and study the Bible passage thoroughly beforehand, grasping its themes and applying its teachings for yourself. Pray that the Holy Spirit will "guide you into truth" so that your leadership will guide others.

2. If the studyguide's questions ever seem ambiguous or unnatural to you, rephrase them, feeling free to add others that seem necessary to bring out the meaning of a verse.

3. Begin (and end) the study promptly. Start by asking someone to pray for God's help. Remember, the Holy Spirit is the teacher, not you!

4. Ask for volunteers to read the passages out loud.

5. As you ask the studyguide's questions in sequence, encourage everyone to participate in the discussion. If some are silent, ask, "What do you think, Heather?" or, "Dan, what can you add to that answer?" or suggest, "Let's have an answer from someone who hasn't spoken up yet."

6. If a question comes up that you can't answer, don't be afraid to admit that you're baffled! Assign the topic as a research project for someone to report on next week.

7. Keep the discussion moving and focused. Though tangents will inevitably be introduced, you can bring the discussion back to the topic at hand. Learn to pace the discussion so that you finish a study each session you meet.

8. Don't be afraid of silences: some questions take time to answer and some people need time to gather courage to speak. If silence persists, rephrase your question, but resist the temptation to answer it yourself.

9. If someone comes up with an answer that is clearly illogical or unbiblical, ask him or her for further clarification: "What verse suggests that to you?"

10. Discourage Bible-hopping and overuse of cross-references. Learn all you can from *this* passage, along with a few important references suggested in the studyguide.

11. Some questions are marked with a ♦. This indicates that further information is available in the Leader's Notes at the back of the guide.

12. For further information on getting a new Bible study group started and keeping it functioning effectively, read Gladys Hunt's *You Can Start a Bible Study Group* and *Pilgrims in Progress: Growing through Groups* by Jim and Carol Plueddemann.

SUGGESTIONS FOR GROUP MEMBERS

1. Learn and apply the following ground rules for effective Bible study. (If new members join the group later, review these guidelines with the whole group.)

2. Remember that your goal is to learn all that you can *from the Bible passage being studied.* Let it speak for itself without using Bible commentaries or other Bible passages. There is more than enough in each assigned passage to keep your group productively occupied for one session. Sticking to the passage saves the group from insecurity and confusion.

3. Avoid the temptation to bring up those fascinating tangents that don't really grow out of the passage you are discussing. If the topic is of common interest, you can bring it up later in informal conversation following the study. Meanwhile, help each other stick to the subject!

4. Encourage each other to participate. People remember best what they discover and verbalize for themselves. Some people are naturally shyer than others, or they may be afraid of making a mistake. If your discussion is free and friendly and you show real interest in what other group members think and feel, they will be more likely to speak up. Remember, the more people involved in a discussion, the richer it will be.

5. Guard yourself from answering too many questions or talking too much. Give others a chance to express themselves. If you are one who participates easily, discipline yourself by counting to ten before you open your mouth!

6. Make personal, honest applications and commit yourself to letting God's Word change you.

ABRAHAM, THE FRIEND OF GOD

Hebrews 11:8-19

Many men do not have deep friendships with other men. However, men who are spiritually mature are likely to be different. As men mature in Christ, they become like Christ who is "the friend who is closer than a brother." Like Christ, they become willing to pray with other men, to make themselves vulnerable to other men, and to express their love to other men.

How fitting, therefore, to begin this studyguide with a man who is remembered for his spiritual maturity. James tells us that Abraham was called "the friend of God." What an honor! No one else in Scripture is given this distinction. And in being a friend of God, Abraham was enabled, as we will see in the next study, to be a true friend to others. In this study, discover exactly why Abraham earned the right to be called God's friend.

1. Pair off and ask your partner questions that will help you get to know him or her. Then go around the room and have each person introduce their partner to the group.

Read Hebrews 11:8-19.

♦ **2.** What is the first "faith" experience of Abraham that the writer of Hebrews describes (verses 8-10)?

How did Abraham respond to this experience, and what did Abraham believe about God that caused him to respond this way?

3. Abraham lived in tents, looking forward to his permanent home. Material things can take time, energy, and devotion. Have you observed how a loose grip on material things can strengthen your relationships with others? If so, share an example.

4. What is the next faith experience which Abraham shared with Sarah? What might have been challenging about this experience?

How did Abraham respond to this experience, and what did Abraham believe about God that caused him to respond this way?

5. The writer of Hebrews elaborates on the kind of attitude Abraham possessed in verses 13-14. What do you learn about being a friend of God from this passage?

◆ **6.** What does being a pilgrim, an alien, a stranger on earth mean to you? How would a commitment to these roles affect your daily life?

More specifically, how might a temporary mindset affect your relationship with those close to you?

7. What is the last faith experience of Abraham described in this passage of Hebrews? What might have been challenging about this experience?

How did Abraham respond to this experience, and what did he believe about God that caused him to respond this way?

8. Jesus tells us in John 8:56 that Abraham "rejoiced at the thought of seeing my day; he saw it and was glad." What are some truths about Christ that you see clearly?

9. How does your faith in those truths affect your actions?

◆ **10.** If possible, briefly share a faith experience of your own, and how you responded to it.

How did your beliefs about God affect that response?

11. If a person has a strong relationship with God, that relationship influences the way he or she relates to friends. If possible, share an example of how your own friendships have been affected by your personal beliefs. How do your beliefs influence your reactions to people, the way you minister to them, etc.?

ABRAHAM, THE FRIEND OF OTHERS

Selections from Genesis 13–21

Sociologists tell us that the primary drive for women is connection, whereas the primary drive for men is status. This is one of the reasons women tend to have more intimate friendships than do men. Women naturally long for connection and are willing to make themselves vulnerable to achieve it. For men, however, vulnerability often threatens their status, so they tend to shy away from intimacy. However, as men mature in Christ and find their security and identity in him, they are more willing to be vulnerable with others.

Abraham is a beautiful example of this, as we will see both in his friendship with Lot and his friendship with his wife, Sarah.

1. If you are a man, share how your own spiritual maturity has affected your willingness to be vulnerable and intimate with others. If you are a woman, describe how you have seen that happening in a man you know.

Read Genesis 13.

2. What problem developed between Abraham's herdsmen and Lot's herdsmen (verses 2, 5-7)?

3. What solution did Abraham propose (verse 9)? How
could this solution possibly have meant a loss in status for
Abraham?

4. Why then, did Abraham propose such a solution
(verse 8), and what does this tell you about his priorities?

What was Lot's response (verses 10-11)? What does this
tell you about his priorities?

♦ **5.** What was the eventual outcome for Abraham (verses 14-17)?

We see from Genesis 14:10-12 what happened to Lot:

> Now the Valley of Siddim was full of tar pits, and when the kings of Sodom and Gomorrah fled, some of the men fell into them and the rest fled to the hills. The four kings seized all the goods of Sodom and Gomorrah and all their food: then they went away. They also carried off Abram's nephew Lot and his possessions, since he was living in Sodom.

How might these outcomes be related to Abraham's and Lot's priorities?

6. What principle did Abraham demonstrate that you can apply in conflicts with others?

Read Genesis 18.

7. How do you see Abraham exercising sensitivity and hospitality in verses 1-8?

8. We see God's intimacy with Abraham in verses 9-22. What promise, thoughts, and revelation can you find from God in this passage?

♦ **9.** How do you see Abraham being a true friend to Lot in verses 22-33?

How could you better follow Abraham's example?

10. Share a time when you interceded in prayer for a friend or a friend interceded for you and you saw God work.

Read Genesis 21:9-21.

11. What happened in this passage? Put yourself in Abraham's place. What feelings do you imagine he was having?

12. To whom did God tell Abraham to submit? Why might this have been difficult?

Why, then, did Abraham obey? What was the result?

13. Repeatedly, Abraham chose to trust and obey God. Sometimes this meant a loss of status, or an attitude of servant-ministry, or personal pain. Yet God blessed Abraham mightily—and one of God's blessings to Abraham was a strong marriage and strong friendships. What have you learned from the model of Abraham that you think God is calling you to apply to your life?

If time permits, pair off and intercede for one another in prayer.

RUTH, A COMMITTED FRIEND

Selections from Ruth

Ruth, a Moabite, chose to leave her homeland to be a companion to her grieving Hebrew mother-in-law, who had lost her husband and sons in Moab. They traveled to Bethlehem, where the people were impressed by Ruth's steadfast love and called her "a woman of excellence."

God is very pleased when we show unfailing love in friendship, as Ruth did. God responded to Ruth's faith and love with an outpouring of love from God's people. As Jesus said in Luke 6:38: "Give, and it will be given to you. A good measure, pressed down, shaken together and running over, will be poured into your lap. For with the measure you use, it will be measured to you."

1. If you have moved to a new city, as Ruth did, share a way God's people reached out to you. Or, share a way you have reached out to someone new in town.

Read Ruth 1.

♦ **2.** Describe the situation in the opening seven verses of Ruth.

3. What evidence do you find that Naomi had shown love to her daughters-in-law, despite the fact that they did not worship the one true God (verses 7-10)?

If you are a parent and your child marries someone who does not worship your God, how will you respond, and why?

4. Describe Naomi's argument and emotions in verses 11-15.

5. What choice does Orpah make? Using your imagination, tell why you think Orpah chose not to commit herself to Naomi and to Naomi's God.

How do you think this choice impacted her eternally?

6. What six promises does Ruth make to Naomi (verses 16-17)?

How do you think this choice impacted Ruth eternally?

7. How did Naomi respond to this commitment? Why do you think Naomi responded as she did?

8. Naomi is in high-tide grief. When you have faced grief, what responses from friends were helpful? Unhelpful?

How does Ruth model a helpful response?

Read Ruth 2–4 silently for an overview.

♦ **9.** What were a few of the ways God showed Ruth his unfailing kindness after her commitment to him? (Find at least one evidence of his care in each chapter.)

10. When Ruth returned from gleaning, how did she include Naomi (2:18)?

How do you feel when a friend trusts you with intimate details about his or her life? Why does this kind of sharing strengthen friendships?

11. What prayer did the friends of Boaz offer for Boaz and Ruth (4:11-12)? How did God answer that prayer?

12. What did the women of Bethlehem think of Ruth (4:15)? What were some of the things that made Ruth such an impressive friend?

♦ **13.** What have you learned from the people in the book of Ruth that will influence how you relate to others? Be specific.

JONATHAN AND DAVID
Soulmates

Selections from 1 Samuel 14; 17–20

Of all the friendships in Scripture, that of David and Jonathan is the best known. These men provide a valuable example for men, modeling the value of godly male friendships. David and Jonathan helped one another reach God's calling for their lives.

David and Jonathan also provide an important model for women who tend to depend upon their relationships rather than on God. David and Jonathan knew the secret of intimacy without dependency: they helped each other find strength in God (1 Samuel 23:16).

In this first study of David and Jonathan, we will consider how God would have us find soulmates, view soulmates, and keep soulmates.

1. What strengths do you think soulmate friendships have that other good friendships lack? What dangers?

Read 1 Samuel 14:6-14.

2. What do you learn about Jonathan's faith from this passage?

3. How did Jonathan's armor-bearer feel about Jonathan (verse 7)?

Read 1 Samuel 17:26-50.

4. What do you learn about David's faith from this passage?

5. How did David's brothers feel about David?

Read 1 Samuel 18:1-4.

6. How do we see God's sensitivity to David's needs by bringing Jonathan into his life?

Can you share a time when you were in need and God brought a friend into your life?

◆ **7.** On the basis of verse 1, find two characteristics of a soulmate. What is the difference between best friends and soulmates?

◆ **8.** What evidence can you find in this passage for Jonathan's faith? How did God seem to be leading him?

Do you look at the people whom God brings across your path with sensitivity to his leading? To what things do you think a Christian should be alert?

9. Have you ever prayed for God to give you a soulmate? If so, what happened?

Read 1 Samuel 18:5-9 and 19:1-7.

10. Describe the first test to David and Jonathan's friendship. How did Jonathan respond?

11. What can you learn from Jonathan from this passage to apply to your life?

Read 1 Samuel 20:1-4.

12. About what did David and Jonathan disagree?

◆ **13.** What do you learn about how well Jonathan listened to David in this disagreement? About Jonathan's character?

When you have a disagreement with a friend, how do you think God would have you respond? Give scriptural support if you can.

14. The words Jonathan spoke to David in verse 4 are the same words Ruth spoke to Naomi in Ruth 3:5. In both cases the difficult request was made by a close friend. Do you see any significance in the similar responses of Ruth and Jonathan? Any application?

15. Studies show that soulmate friendships can usually pass the tests of distance or stress, but often die when subjected to the test of hurt feelings. Why do you think this is? How could we respond in a way that is more pleasing to God?

JONATHAN AND DAVID
Covenant Friends

1 Samuel 20; 23:15-18; 2 Samuel 9;
Ecclesiastes 5:1-7

Isn't it interesting that, as in the relationship between Ruth and Naomi, so now with David and Jonathan, a friendship promise is made? Is it possible that a friendship vow can hold together a soulmate friendship in difficult times in the same way a marriage vow can hold together a marriage in difficult times? Ruth and Naomi's friendship lasted—as did David and Jonathan's. Very few friendships last until death. So a covenant friendship is an intriguing idea—but it certainly isn't something to be entered into hastily.

1. What is the value of marriage vows? The danger?

Read 1 Samuel 20 before your group meets.

2. In a sentence, what was David and Jonathan's plan? How did it work out?

3. Describe the covenant made in verses 12-17.

Often, when a new king came to power, the old king's family was slaughtered by the new reign. What additional light does this shed on the covenant?

4. Describe the parting scene between David and Jonathan (verses 41-42).

How did Jonathan give David the strength to leave him? What was he really saying?

5. Shakespeare said, "Parting is such sweet sorrow." Have you found this to be true? What is the value of parting scenes?

Read 1 Samuel 23:15-18.

6. How was Jonathan demonstrating faithfulness to David in this passage?

♦ **7.** Maturity in friendship is demonstrated when one helps the other "find strength in God" rather than in himself or herself. How do you think Jonathan did this for David in the wilderness?

List some ways you could do this for your friends. Then choose one and do it! What do you plan to do?

Read 2 Samuel 9 before your group meets.

♦ **8.** Describe how, after Jonathan's death, David is still keeping his covenant with him.

9. This is a beautiful symbolic passage. Can you see any parallels with our relationship to God?

Read Ecclesiastes 5:1-7.

10. Find at least five warnings concerning making vows to God.

What would be the value of making a friendship covenant as David and Jonathan did? The danger?

11. If you have entered into a friendship covenant with someone, share something about it.

12. Review the characteristics of friendship as revealed in the lives of David and Jonathan.

♦ 13. (For personal reflection) There is "a time to keep and a time to throw away" (Ecclesiastes 3:6). Sometimes God gives us friendships for a season, and then allows them to drift away so that there is room in our lives for new friendships. It takes prayer and discernment to know if God is calling you to be faithful to a friend for life. If God calls you to be true to a friend, you should be, whether or not you have made a vow. As you are still before him, to whom is he calling you to be faithful? What wisdom does he give you?

SOLOMON, SON OF DAVID

Selected verses from Solomon's writings

As in other areas of our development, we learn the meaning of friendship from the people who are our models in childhood. In Proverbs 4:3-4, Solomon says, "When I was a boy in my father's house, still tender, and an only child of my mother, he taught me and said, 'Lay hold of my words with all your heart; keep my commands and you will live.'" It seems that King David made an effort to teach his young son principles of good living.

Since Solomon succeeded David to the throne, it is likely that he was familiar with the palace when he was a child. He undoubtedly knew the story behind the crippled Mephibosheth, who ate at the king's table, and this communicated something to young Solomon about friendship. Friendship was a subject that captured Solomon's attention as he wrote and collected his famous proverbs, which we find in the books of Proverbs and Ecclesiastes.

1. What models of friendship have you had in your life? What kindnesses or courtesies have you incorporated into your life because of those models? Be as specific as possible.

Read Ecclesiastes 4:9-12.

2. What are some of the values of friendship (or marriage) that Solomon lists in this passage?

Have you experienced any of these specific benefits? If so, share.

3. What do you think a cord of three strands is? How was this metaphor true in the friendship between David and Jonathan?

4. Did you help a friend find strength in God last week? What did you do?

5. Solomon says: "A friend loves at all times, and a brother is born for adversity" (Proverbs 17:17).

What have been the most helpful things friends have done for you in adversity?

6. Proverbs 25:20 says, "Like one who takes away a garment on a cold day, or like vinegar poured on soda, is one who sings songs to a heavy heart."

What might be harmful to a friend who is hurting?

7. Solomon says: "Many a man claims to have unfailing love, but a faithful man who can find?" (Proverbs 20:6).

What might be some reasons that a friend would fail to come through when you need him most?

How does understanding this help you to forgive a friend who has failed?

8. Proverbs 10:12 says: "Hatred stirs up dissension, but love covers over all wrongs."

What will a lack of forgiveness do to a friendship? To yourself? To the glory of God?

◆ **9.** When there is a grievance between you and a friend, who should be the peacemaker?

10. Proverbs 25:17 says: "Seldom set foot in your neighbor's house—too much of you, and he will hate you."

What are some of the dangers of being dependent on only one friend? How much contact is too much?

For this last segment of the study, break into groups of three or four.

11. Proverbs 16:24 says: "Pleasant words are a honey-comb, sweet to the soul and healing to the bones."

Take turns affirming one another by sharing some of the godly characteristics you see in one another's lives.

12. Meditate on the following proverbs:

> The purposes of a man's heart are deep waters, but a man of understanding draws them out. (Proverbs 20:5)

> Perfume and incense bring joy to the heart, and the pleasantness of one's friend springs from his earnest counsel. (Proverbs 27:9)

> As iron sharpens iron, so one man sharpens another. (Proverbs 27:17)

What are some of the truths that strike you from these proverbs?

♦ **13.** List some questions that might help you "draw out" the heart of a friend (Proverbs 20:5).

Now pray, conversationally, for one another.

SOLOMON'S FOLLY
The Failure to Apply Wisdom

Selected verses from Proverbs; 1 Kings 9:1-9; 11:1-13

As the parents of five children, we have seen the tremendous influence of friends. We are not surprised by one study that showed the most reliable predictor of a teenager's sexual activity to be the sexual activity of his or her closest friends. The Lord impressed on our hearts the importance of helping our children become friends with children from godly homes when they were very young. Our children have been strengthened greatly as a result of these friendships.

Solomon gives many warnings about being cautious in friendship and of how friends can corrupt us. He also says that the wise man listens carefully to advice. Yet Solomon failed to heed his own proverbs, shutting his ears to the warnings of God. This led to great sorrow and waste in Solomon's life.

1. Think about the friendships of your youth. How did they influence you for good or for evil? How about your friendships now?

2. Read the following warnings from Proverbs:

> A righteous man is cautious in friendship, but the way of the wicked leads them astray. (Proverbs 12:26)

> He who walks with the wise grows wise, but a companion of fools suffers harm. (Proverbs 13:20)

> Do not make friends with a hot-tempered man, do not associate with one easily angered, or you may learn his ways and get yourself ensnared. (Proverbs 22:24-25)

What common theme runs throughout the above proverbs? What particular points stand out to you and why?

3. Without mentioning names, what friends in your life today have the potential of leading you astray? How might you guard your heart?

4. Proverbs 4:14-15 says:

> Do not set foot on the path of the wicked or walk in the way of evil men. Avoid it, do not travel on it; turn from it and go on your way.

God clearly wants us to be friends with non-Christians, as Jesus was, yet not to walk their "path." Give some examples of how you might become a friend to a non-Christian and yet graciously refuse to walk on a path he or she has chosen.

5. Solomon also warned concerning friendships with the opposite sex—not only with immoral women, but about becoming involved sexually with your future spouse before the time is right. Three times we are told:

> **Do not arouse or awaken love until it so desires. (Song of Songs 2:7; 3:5; 8:4)**

Why do you think God insists that we confine sexual involvement to marriage? How far is too far?

♦ **6.** Do you think a married person should allow himself or herself to be close friends with someone of the opposite sex? Explain.

Read 1 Kings 9:1-9.

7. Describe what happened here when the Lord appeared to Solomon. Take time to notice several details. What did Solomon have to gain by obedience? To lose by disobedience?

8. Can you share a time in your life when the alternatives of obedience and disobedience were especially clear to you?

Read 1 Kings 11:1-13.

9. Why did God tell the Israelites not to marry unbelieving women (verse 2)? Why is it so difficult to hold firm to the Lord when someone connected to you is against it?

What are some other "gods" to which a contemporary unbelieving spouse might turn a believer's heart?

10. How many wives did Solomon have (verse 3)? What happened because of these marriages (verses 3-4)?

There are many warnings to young people about the dangers of bad company, but it is clear that older people can be vulnerable to the influence of bad company as well. When was Solomon's heart impacted (verse 4)?

11. What was God's reaction to Solomon's backsliding (verse 9)? What significance do you see in the mentioning of the point that God had been especially good to Solomon, appearing to him twice?

Name a way the Lord has been especially good to you.
How should this impact your trust and obedience?

12. Are there some specific areas in your life in which
God has made his will clear to you? What are they?

What steps do you need to take to avoid disobeying God
in your friendships? What might be the consequences of
obedience or disobedience?

MARY AND ELIZABETH
God Meets Needs through Friendship

Luke 1:5-80

God provided Elizabeth as the perfect mentor to Mary. Elizabeth was a godly woman who knew exactly how to encourage Mary. For three months Elizabeth showed hospitality to Mary, giving her an opportunity to watch a godly wife in action. And since Elizabeth was a little more than six months pregnant when Mary arrived, and Mary stayed three months, it makes sense to us that Mary was there for the birth of John the Baptist. Mary didn't know that she was going to give birth on a bare barn floor—but God knew, and we believe that perhaps he provided her with hands-on experience in watching the delivery of Elizabeth's baby, the tying of the umbilical cord, and the wrapping of the infant in swaddling clothes. God knew Mary's needs better than she did. And he prepared her, through friendship, for the difficult road ahead.

1. Friends can be a surprise gift from God. Has God ever surprised you with the gift of a friend? Why do you think God was involved?

Read Luke 1:5-80 on your own.

2. Tell what you find in each of the following verses that would pave the way for rapport between Mary and Elizabeth:

verses 6 and 30

verses 13 and 30-31

verses 15 and 32

verses 19 and 26

verse 36

verse 41

3. Gathering clues from verses 6 and 25, how do you think Elizabeth felt about her barrenness? Had it made her bitter or better? Support your answer.

Read Luke 1:34-45 aloud.

♦ **4.** What reasons can you think of for God telling Mary about Elizabeth?

Why do you think Mary *hurried* to go and see Elizabeth?

5. Find several ways Elizabeth encouraged Mary in verses 42-45.

6. In what ways do you think Mary's visit was an encouragement to Elizabeth?

7. What difference might Elizabeth have seen between Zechariah's (verses 18-20) and Mary's (verse 45) faith?

8. How do you think Elizabeth's words in verses 42-45 helped Mary find strength in God?

How do you think three months with a godly older woman benefited Mary?

9. Elizabeth was "well along in years," and Mary was the age at which girls were pledged in marriage, probably her mid-teens. Do you think age was a barrier or a benefit in the friendship between these two women? What dynamics would age difference bring to their relationship?

10. Have you been blessed by being on either the younger or older side of a mentoring friendship? If so, share.

11. What are some specific ways you could reach out in friendship, as Elizabeth did, to younger Christians in your life? To older? Be specific.

12. After Elizabeth encouraged Mary in the Lord, Mary was inspired to give her "Magnificat" (verses 46-55). What are some things Mary believed wholeheartedly?

♦ **13.** What similar thought seemed to overwhelm both Elizabeth (verse 25) and Mary (verse 48)? Share a time when you were aware that the Lord was mindful of you. How did you feel?

JESUS, THE HIGHEST MODEL OF FRIENDSHIP

Matthew 26:36-56; Luke 5:27-32

During his earthly life, Jesus modeled friendship perfectly. He was vulnerable and committed, practiced forgiveness, and loved others tenaciously. He also modeled the importance of being a friend to sinners. And we are told to walk in his steps.

1. Could you write an essay entitled, "Jesus—My Friend"? If so, what stories would you put in it? (Share one briefly with the group.)

Read Matthew 26:36-56.

2. What friendship qualities do you see in Jesus in this passage? (Give Scripture references.)

How could you follow in Jesus' steps?

3. Commitment in friendship can be costly. How is this seen in this passage?

4. Jesus, being fully man as well as fully God, had the same needs for friendship as we do. How did Jesus make himself vulnerable to his friends?

♦ **5.** When men share openly and make themselves vulnerable, do they become more or less manly in your eyes? Why?

6. Why are people often hesitant to be completely honest about their needs? To ask for help? To ask for prayers?

♦ **7.** What are some personal needs in your life right now?

8. What did Jesus do when his friends let him down (verses 40-44)?

♦ **9.** What are your reactions when you make yourself vulnerable and your friend lets you down, even repeatedly?

How could you become more forgiving of your friends?

10. John 15:13 says: "Greater love has no one than this, that he lay down his life for his friends." Though most of us won't be asked literally to die for our friends, still, in every genuine friendship, some kind of death, of dying to self, is required. Read the following Scriptures and then explain, possibly with an example, how a friend, because of his commitment to another, might die to self.

> A friend loves at all times, and a brother is born for adversity. (Proverbs 17:17)

> [Love] is not rude, it is not self-seeking, it is not easily angered, it keeps no record of wrongs. (1 Corinthians 13:5)

> Confess your sins to each other and pray for each other so that you may be healed. (James 5:16)

> If anyone has material possessions and sees his
> brother in need but has no pity on him, how can the
> love of God be in him? (1 John 3:17)

Read Luke 5:27-32.

11. Of what were the Pharisees critical in Jesus? What
was his response? What did he mean?

12. Jesus was called a friend of sinners. His mercy caused
him to reach out to those most in need of him. How could
you follow in Jesus' steps?

What goal could you set for yourself as a "friend of sinners" and be accountable for in this study group?

BARNABAS, SON OF ENCOURAGEMENT

Acts 4:32-37; 9:17-31

Before Gethsemane, Jesus prayed that there would be such harmony and love between believers that the world would be convinced that the Father had indeed sent the Son (John 17:20-23). Barnabas is a model to us of the kind of friend Jesus prayed for: a man who grasped the importance of peace and love between believers. Because of that understanding, Barnabas did all he could to encourage harmony and love.

1. Share briefly about a person in your life who believed in you and, in so doing, helped you to be more of what God intended you to be. How did he or she encourage you?

Read Acts 4:32-37.

♦ **2.** What distinguishing characteristics do you find in this group of believers? What could we learn from them?

3. What name did the apostles call Joseph (verse 36)? What did the name mean? Using your imagination, describe the character and lifestyle of someone meriting the name "Son of Encouragement."

4. What was Barnabas's first recorded act of encouragement (verse 37)?

In what ways could you follow Barnabas's example here?

5. How would the general atmosphere or tone of this fellowship group help Barnabas to be an encourager?

Read Acts 9:17-31.

6. Why didn't the believers trust Saul?

7. Who came to his defense in verse 27, and how?

8. Compare Barnabas's approach in defending Saul with Jonathan's approach in defending David (1 Samuel 19:4-5). What do you learn from these models about being a peacemaker?

9. If it is clear to you that a person loves God and is committed to the Christian lifestyle, and yet there are believers who are distrustful of him or her, why would it be important for you to be a friend to that person?

Can you share a time when you were either the giver or recipient of such kindness?

10. What can be difficult about being a peacemaker? Why do you think Barnabas bothered to get involved with Saul?

What was the result for the early church (verse 31)?

11. Jesus said, "Blessed are the peacemakers, for they will be called sons of God." Why do you think peacemakers merit this title?

◆ **12.** Is there a situation coming up this week in which you could apply the principles of encouragement or peacemaking you have seen in Barnabas's life? What do you plan to do?

BARNABAS'S LATER MINISTRY

Selections from Acts 11–15

In Acts 11, Barnabas rejoiced when he saw "evidence of the grace of God" and proclaimed it! Though he was not the one who initially proclaimed the gospel in Antioch, he was not jealous but overjoyed that it had been proclaimed and believed. Full of excitement, he made the long journey to Antioch to see this good work. Upon seeing it firsthand, his enthusiasm waved the flames of excitement even higher, and many more people were brought to the Lord.

Barnabas also gives us an example, in Acts 15, of standing by a believer who has failed. It has been said that Christians shoot their wounded. How we need to learn from Barnabas.

1. In this Bible study group, what evidence of God's grace have you seen? Answers to prayer? Wisdom gleaned? Love for one another?

Read Acts 11:19-30.

2. Why do you think Barnabas agreed to make the long trip from Jerusalem to Antioch?

Are you excited about the work being done for Christ by other believers? How might you encourage them and fan their flames?

3. What was evident to Barnabas when he arrived in Antioch (verse 23)? What kinds of things do you think he saw?

4. How did he react?

How might you encourage believers in your life to "remain true to the Lord with all their hearts"?

5. What three things do you learn about Barnabas in verse 24? How did these characteristics help him to be an encourager?

6. Why did Barnabas go to Tarsus (verse 25)? Do you think Barnabas was a good team worker? What makes a good team worker?

Read Acts 15:25-26 and 36-41.

7. Why did Paul want to exclude John Mark from the second missionary journey (verses 37-38)? What things do you imagine might have been said by Paul? By Barnabas?

♦ **8.** Paul may very well have been right not to trust John Mark with this responsibility at this point. Yet had it not been for Barnabas, the blow to John Mark could have been fatal. How can we encourage believers who have failed (whether in ministry, marriage, integrity) without causing harm to the work of Christ? If possible, give an example.

♦ **9.** In 2 Timothy 4:11, we see that Paul later had a change of heart and wrote, "Get Mark and bring him with you, because he is helpful to me in my ministry." What do we learn about Mark here? How do you suppose Barnabas contributed to the change?

10. Why is it important not to give up on our friends when they disappoint us (as Barnabas stood by Mark)? Why is it important to reconcile with friends after we have differences (as Barnabas/Paul/Mark)? What will be the result for the church?

Closing Thoughts

◆ **11.** What characteristics of good friendships have you dis-
covered in these models of God's family album? Have
each group member share at least one characteristic.

12. What do you expect to remember from this studyguide on friendship that will make a difference in your
life? What is already making a difference?

LEADER'S NOTES

■ **Study 1/Abraham, the Friend of God**

Question 2. In this call, Abraham was converted from the idolatry of his father's house.

Question 6. Take some time with this, encouraging group members to dig into this important passage. You might draw members out further by asking them to describe the perspective of a pilgrim, some of the things they think these people "saw," and God's feeling about these people.

Question 10. If time permits, go around the circle with this to hear from everyone. However, give them the freedom to pass.

■ **Study 2/Abraham, the Friend of Others**

Question 5. Though Sodom was lush, her people were sinful. Choosing Sodom might have meant a temporary elevation in status for Lot, but it was shortsighted both for him and for his family. Ezekiel 16:49 tells us: "Now this was the sin of your sister Sodom: She and her daughters were arrogant, overfed and unconcerned; they did not help the poor and needy." In the end Sodom was destroyed by God, and Lot and his family had to be rescued by God's intervention (see Genesis 19).

Question 9. Oswald Chambers commented: "We see where other people are failing, and then we take our discernment and turn it into comments of ridicule and criticism, instead of turning it into intercession on their behalf." Abraham is a model of intercession instead of criticism! (Oswald Chambers, *My Utmost for His Highest,* devotional for March 31. Grand Rapids: Discovery House, 1992).

Study 3/Ruth, a Committed Friend

Question 2. Deuteronomy 11:13-17 tells us that God promised that there would not be a famine in the Promised Land unless his people had turned from him. Obviously this, therefore, was the case in the opening verses of Ruth—and God was looking for repentance from his people. Instead of repenting, Elimelech took his family to idol-worshipping Moab. Most commentators believe Elimelech's death in Moab was the judgment of God. The sons then married women who did not worship the one true God. In 1 Kings 11:1-4, in the story of Solomon and his Moabite wives, we are told that God had warned the Israelites not to marry foreign wives because they would turn their hearts to other gods. Many commentators feel that the sons' deaths were the judgment of God as well.

Question 9. God had established some laws to help people who had suffered misfortune and material setbacks. One was that gleanings were to be left for those in need (Deuteronomy 24:19). Another was the perpetuation of a brother's name: if a man died (as Ruth's husband had died) and left her with no children (Ruth had been barren in Moab), then the brother or a near kinsman was to marry her and raise up the first son in his late kinsman's name (Deuteronomy 25:5-10). The fact that Ruth "happened" to begin gleaning in the field of a man related to her late husband is a very strong evidence of God's providential care.

Question 13. If time permits, hear from everyone, giving them the freedom to pass.

■ Study 4/Jonathan and David: Soulmates

Question 7. "Jonathan became one in spirit," not in body, "with David" (1 Samuel 18:1). David and Jonathan have been accused of being homosexuals, but there is no evidence for this. This practice was strictly forbidden in Hebrew culture. Furthermore, God expressed approval of David's life, with the exception of the incident of adultery with Bathsheba and the murder of her husband Uriah (1 Kings 15:5), which the Lord brought into the open and dealt with. If David had committed a sin as serious as homosexuality, this likely would not have been hidden from record. In modern Western culture, sex has become so central to our concept of relationship that we have difficulty perceiving intimacy without it. Yet close, affectionate friendship between men has not been an oddity in other cultures, including the early Hebrew culture that is the setting for this story.

Question 8. Jonathan was next in line to be king of Israel. His actions show he was willing to step aside because he thought David was the man in God's plan. He was giving him his robe, the robe of the next king of Israel.

Question 13. It takes a godly person to listen with hearing ears when a friend disagrees with you—particularly when he or she is saying negative things about you or someone you love. Yet Scripture tells us that the wise man listens carefully to criticism (Proverbs 9:8; 18:2; 27:6).

■ Study 5/Jonathan and David: Covenant Friends

Question 7. Some ways to help a friend find strength in God are by praying with him, telling him ways you have seen God at work in his life, ministering together with him, sharing Scripture with him, sharing a testimony of God's faithfulness to you, or giving him a Christian book. Hear from everyone and tell them that they will be held accountable next week for doing something!

Question 8. Mephibosheth's nurse fled with him when he was a baby and David became king, because she assumed he would be slaughtered. As she ran, she tripped and he became crippled. Though David was slow to keep his promise, he does keep it, as demonstrated in this chapter.

Question 13. Some helpful questions to ask when doing this exercise are: With whom an I one in spirit? Has he or she shown a desire to be faithful to me? How is God leading?

■ Study 6/Solomon, Son of David

Question 9. If you are a believer and there is a grievance between you and a friend, it's always your turn to go and do whatever you can to be at peace with them (Matthew 5:23-24). It takes maturity to be genuinely forgiving and kind rather than vengeful.

Question 13. If the group is unfamiliar with conversational prayer, prepare them by explaining that, as in conversation, you talk about one subject at a time. In this situation, pray about one person at a time. And then, when people have stopped lifting up short sentence prayers about that person, pray for the next person.

■ Study 7/Solomon's Folly: The Failure to Apply Wisdom

Question 6. This is an opinion question. Author and radio speaker Karen Mains has said that she thinks friendships between married men and women are possible as long as they keep Christ between them. This seems wise to us, and along with that it seems prudent to be guarded about physical contact and conversation about sexual things. In discipleship ministries, such as the Navigators, it is recommended that men disciple men and women disciple women. Solomon does say, "Can a man scoop fire into his lap without his clothes being burned?" (Proverbs 6:27). Certainly caution is called for in opposite-sex friendships, but it seems to us that, in Christ, it is possible. However, if you feel yourself being attracted, our advice is to flee.

■ Study 8/Mary and Elizabeth: God Meets Needs through Friendship

Question 4. In part, this news encouraged Mary that miracles are possible. But it also seems that God wanted Mary to go and see Elizabeth and therefore put that desire in her heart, for he knew she was going to need someone who would understand and encourage her.

Question 13. If time permits, hear from everyone, giving people the freedom to pass.

■ Study 9/Jesus, the Highest Model of Friendship

Question 5. It takes more courage to be vulnerable than to be remote, to accept help when you need it. Spiritually mature men in the Scriptures had the courage to ask for and receive help (Moses: Exodus 18:17-24; Paul: 2 Timothy 4:9-22).

Question 7. Hopefully this will lead to some honest sharing. You may need to be an example by sharing vulnerably. You may want to follow this question with a brief time of prayer for one another, perhaps by clustering in threes. Or, if one person shares vulnerably you may feel led, right then, to ask a few members to say sentence prayers for her or him.

Question 9. Studies show that even Christians have trouble forgiving from their heart. The parable of the unmerciful servant (Matthew 18:21-35) and Ephesians 4:32 encourage us to remember how much Christ has forgiven us and to do likewise!

■ Study 10/Barnabas, Son of Encouragement

Question 2. Commentator Larry Richards says: "No one lost control of his or her own possessions (communism). But each Christian cared more about other persons than material possessions (Christianity)." (Lawrence Richards, *The Bible Reader's Companion,* p. 712. Wheaton, Ill.: Victor, 1991).

Question 12. If time permits, you could spend some time encouraging one another by writing on an index card three things you admire about the person on your right and then giving it to him or her. Or, you can encourage one another verbally, going around the room.

■ Study 11/ Barnabas's Later Ministry

Question 8. It seems wise not to give Christians who have fallen into sin positions of responsibility until it is evident from their life that true repentance has taken place. However, that doesn't mean that we stop loving them or being a friend to them. It may even be appropriate to give them limited responsibility, with some supervision.

Question 9. John Mark later wrote the Gospel of Mark.

Questions 11-12. Leave time in this lesson for these review questions. It would be good to give everyone an opportunity to share.

WHAT SHOULD WE STUDY NEXT?

To help your group answer that question, we've listed the Fisherman Guides by category so you can choose your next study.

TOPICAL STUDIES

Angels, Wright

Becoming a Woman of Wisdom: Insights from Esther, Smith

Becoming Women of Purpose, Barton

Building Your House on the Lord, Brestin

The Creative Heart of God, Goring

Discipleship, Reapsome

Doing Justice, Showing Mercy, Wright

Encouraging Others, Johnson

The End Times, Rusten

Examining the Claims of Jesus, Brestin

Friendship, Brestin

The Fruit of the Spirit, Briscoe

Great Doctrines of the Bible, Board

Great Passages of the Bible, Plueddemann

Great Prayers of the Bible, Plueddemann

Growing Through Life's Challenges, Reapsome

Guidance & God's Will, Stark

Heart Renewal, Goring

Higher Ground, Brestin

Integrity, Engstrom & Larson

Lifestyle Priorities, White

Marriage, Stevens

Miracles, Castleman

One Body, One Spirit, Larson

The Parables of Jesus, Hunt

Prayer, Jones

The Prophets, Wright

Proverbs & Parables, Brestin

Satisfying Work, Stevens & Schoberg

Senior Saints, Reapsome

Sermon on the Mount, Hunt

A Spiritual Legacy, Christensen

Spiritual Warfare, Moreau

The Ten Commandments, Briscoe

Who Is God? Seemuth

Who Is Jesus? Van Reken

Who Is the Holy Spirit? Knuckles & Van Reken

Witnesses to All the World, Plueddemann

Worship, Sibley

BIBLE BOOK STUDIES

Genesis, Fromer & Keyes
Exodus, Larsen
Job, Klug
Psalms, Klug
Proverbs: Wisdom That Works,
   Wright
Jeremiah, Reapsome
Jonah, Habakkuk, & Malachi,
   Fromer & Keyes
Matthew, Sibley
Mark, Christensen
Luke, Keyes
John: Living Word, Kuniholm
Acts 1-12, Christensen
Paul (Acts 13-28), Christiansen
Romans: The Christian
   Story, Reapsome
1 Corinthians, Hummel

Strengthened to Serve
   (2 Corinthians),
   Plueddemann
Galatians, Titus & Philemon,
   Kuniholm
Ephesians, Baylis
Philippians, Klug
Colossians, Shaw
Letters to the Thessalonians,
   Fromer & Keyes
Letters to Timothy, Fromer &
   Keyes
Hebrews, Hunt
James, Christensen
1 & 2 Peter, Jude, Brestin
How Should a Christian Live?
   (1, 2 & 3 John), Brestin
Revelation, Hunt

BIBLE CHARACTER STUDIES

David: Man after God's Own
   Heart, Castleman
Elijah, Castleman
Great People of the Bible,
   Plueddemann
King David: Trusting God for
   a Lifetime, Castleman
Men Like Us, Heidebrecht &
   Scheuermann

Moses, Asimakoupoulos
Paul (Acts 13-28), Christensen
Ruth & Daniel, Stokes
Women Like Us, Barton
Women Who Achieved for
   God, Christensen
Women Who Believed God,
   Christensen

Printed in the United States
by Baker & Taylor Publisher Services